kidpower® safety comics

People Safety Skills for Children Ages 3 to 10

Irene van der Zande
Illustrated by Amanda Golert

relationsafe™
SKILLS FOR LIFELONG SAFETY AND SUCCESS

A publication of Kidpower Teenpower Fullpower International

Copyright And Permission To Use Information

Copyright Information

Reproduction Information

Use of Content for Personal Learning or for Teaching Others

Restrictions

Liability Disclaimer

Kidpower Teenpower Fullpower International
Office   *831-426-4407 or (USA) 1-800-467-6997*
E-mail   *safety@kidpower.org*
Web page   *www.kidpower.org*
Address   *P.O. Box 1212, Santa Cruz, CA 95061, USA*

Table Of Contents

Welcome To Kidpower!

Thank you for learning about People Safety! We use the term "People Safety" to mean people being emotionally and physically safe both with other people and yourself. *Kidpower Safety Comics* is for children ages 3 to 10 who are usually with adults such as parents or teachers who can help them if they have a safety problem. These skills, ideas, and teaching methods are also important for toddlers and teenagers—and for their adults. Reading this book together can help increase safety for the whole family.

The entertaining drawings, clear explanations, and social stories make it fun and easy to understand how to use People Safety skills in daily life. The information for adults describes how to protect children and to support them in learning, practicing, and using these skills. When learning and teaching safety skills, please keep these important ideas in mind:

1. **Learning and practicing People Safety is best done in a way that is fun and useful rather than scary or overwhelming.** Focus on skills and ways to be as safe as possible rather than talking about all the bad things that might happen. Through calm conversations, fun hands-on practice, and enthusiastic encouragement, we can learn how to stay safe most of the time.

2. **People learn better by doing than by being told what to do.** The Discussions and Practices section on pages 51 to 55 describes how to act out the skills that you see the children in the drawings using keep themselves safe. Just like Water Safety, Food Safety, Fire Safety, Bike Safety and Car Safety, making People Safety part of your daily life is important. Encourage each other to be successful.

3. Children are safest when they know they have caring adults in their lives who believe in them and who they can trust to help them when they have a problem. Adults, please make SURE kids know you CARE. Discuss the Kidpower Protection Promise on page 9. No matter how busy you are, occasionally ask children calmly, "Is there anything you have been worrying or wondering about?" Listen to their answers respectfully without lecturing or joking, and thank them for telling you. Notice and focus on what kids are doing right instead of focusing mostly on the ways you want them to change. Tell them often, "I love you just the way you are."

Kidpower teaches kids to use our power to stay safe!

How To Use This Book

Discuss and practice these ideas with your family, school, or
youth group so that everyone has a common understanding about safety.

1. Read the book yourself. Notice how many of these ideas and skills are important for adults too.

2. Discuss the relevant sections of the book with your children. Point out the different ways that children in the stories are solving a variety of People Safety problems.

3. Follow the Discussion and Practices directions on pages 51 to 55 to practice the skills together.

4. Remember to use these skills out in the real world every day.

How Adults Can Help Kids Stay Safe

Keep your radar on, stay in charge, and make and practice safety plans together.

1. Stay calm. Children learn better when their grown-ups are calm.

Stay with me when we cross the street.

2. Remember that children need adult supervision and protection until they have the skills, knowledge, and life experience to keep themselves safe.

Sorry! You have to wait until I can go with you.

3. Make a safety plan for how to get help everywhere you go. The Safety Plan will be different for different people, at different times of the day, and in different places.

BIG STORE

Stay with me, but if you get lost, remember your Safety Plan and go to the checkout counter.

4. Review and practice People Safety skills every day, everywhere.

What do you do if someone knocks on the door?

Find you and Check First!

Knock Knock

A publication of Kidpower Teenpower Fullpower International® www.kidpower.org For permission to copy, contact safety@kidpower.org

More Ways Adults Can Help Kids Stay Safe

Kids learn more from what they do and from what they
see their adults doing than from what they are told to do.

1. Help children be successful in practicing skills by coaching them to handle problems in the moment.

2. Help children understand about strangers. Tell them most people are good, but if they do not know someone well, their Safety Plan is to check with you right away.

3. Set a good example. Solve problems respectfully and powerfully.

4. Listen to children. Respect their feelings, even if their worries seem silly to you.

Kidpower's Underlying Principle
The safety and well-being of a child are more important than *anyone's* embarrassment, inconvenience, or offense.

 A publication of Kidpower Teenpower Fullpower International® www.kidpower.org For permission to copy, contact safety@kidpower.org

Make The kid**power** Protection Promise™

"You are VERY important to me! If you have a safety problem, I want to know. Even if I seem too busy. Or might feel upset. Or don't understand at first. Even if someone we care about will be upset. Even if it is embarrassing. Even if you made a mistake. Please tell me, and I will do everything in my power to help you."

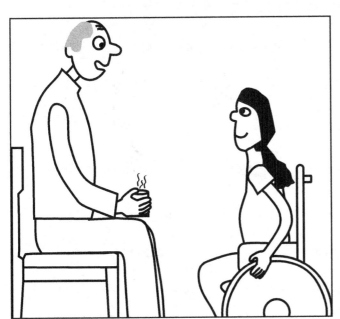

Be Aware, Calm, Respectful, And Confident

People will bother you less and listen to you more when you are looking around; acting calm, respectful, and confident; and staying in control of your body.

1. Stuart is not paying attention and looks scared. This is **less safe**.

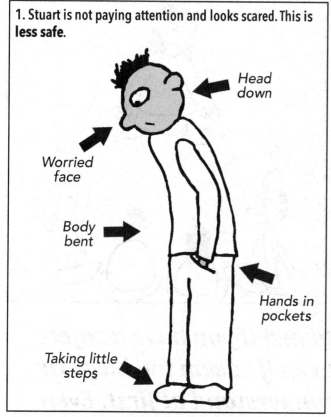

Head down

Worried face

Body bent

Hands in pockets

Taking little steps

2. Stuart looks aware and strong. This is **more safe**.

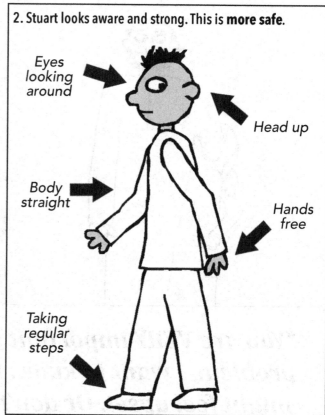

Eyes looking around

Head up

Body straight

Hands free

Taking regular steps

3. Mariah is acting mad. She looks like she wants to fight. This is **less safe**.

Angry face

Yelling rude things

Body out of control

Hitting hands

4. Mariah looks calm, respectful, and confident. This is **more safe**.

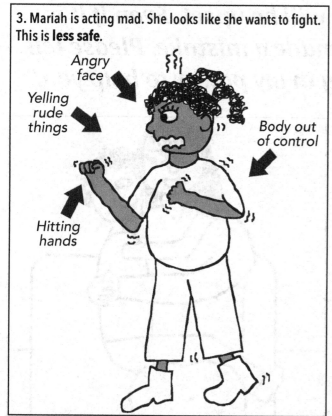

Calm aware face

Thinking, not yelling

Body in control

Hands down

A publication of Kidpower Teenpower Fullpower International® www.kidpower.org For permission to copy, contact safety@kidpower.org

Different Kinds Of Power

We can use our power to think, move, and speak to stay safe and act safely.

1. Rana is rude and sticks out her tongue. Christopher keeps his tongue and words in his mouth by using his *Mouth Closed Power* to stay safe.

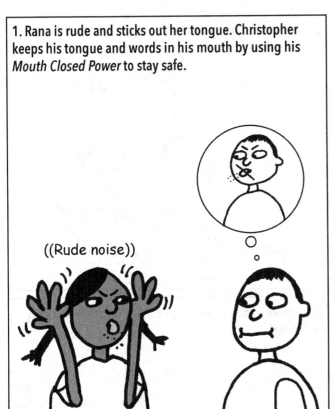

2. Eric hits his big brother. His big brother stops the hit and uses his *Hands Down Power* to keep himself from hitting back.

3. Nancy tries to grab the scooter. Michael uses his *STOP! Power* by having a strong voice and making a fence with his hands so he sounds and looks like he means it.

4. George yells at his friend. His friend does *not* yell back. She uses her *Walk Away Power* to get away from his words and to stay safe.

The Leaving Story

Moving out of reach helps to stop problems from growing bigger.

1. Michelle likes to play with her friend Yoko in the sandbox.

2. When Yoko gets mad and throws things, she can be mean to Michelle too.

3. When Yoko is in a bad mood, Michelle can walk away.

4. Michelle can play with other children, or she can play by herself.

5. To practice moving out of reach, have the child start close to you. Make sure there is room behind the child to back up away from you. Coach the child to look at you and to glance back while backing up.

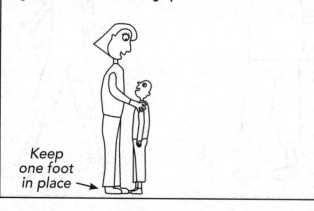

Keep one foot in place →

6. Check to see if the child is out of reach. Coach kids to be successful. Do not grab them if they are too close. Just coach them to move back more.

Keep one foot in place

 A publication of Kidpower Teenpower Fullpower International® www.kidpower.org For permission to copy, contact safety@kidpower.org

The Walk Away Power Story

It is no fun to be pushed when waiting in line. It is more important to be next to someone who is not pushing than to be at the front of the line.

1. Annabelle is pushing in line. Mariela has not done or said anything, but Annabelle is still bothering her.

2. Mariela wishes Annabelle would stop pushing. But she does not notice and pushes more.

3. Mariela gets mad and pushes back. The teacher gets mad at both of them.

4. Next time Annabelle pushes, Mariela leaves the line and finds another place. It is not important to be in front of the line. It is more important to be next to a kid who does not push.

Together Or On Your Own

The rules are different if you are together with
an adult who can help you or if you are on your own.

1. If Christopher is right next to his mom at the store, they are *together*.

Together

2. The storekeeper has free samples. If Christopher's mom gives permission, he can take food from the storekeeper.

Together

3. If Christopher and his mom are away from each other even a little bit, Christopher is on his own. If his mom is in the next aisle and a lady has free samples...

On Your Own

4. Christopher's Safety Plan is to move away and go to his mom so he can *Check First*.

Move Away and Check First

A publication of Kidpower Teenpower Fullpower International® www.kidpower.org For permission to copy, contact safety@kidpower.org

Where Is Safety?

Safety is where you can find adults to help you.

1. Where is safety at my school?

My teacher is safety!

2. Where is safety at my home?

My grown-ups are safety!

3. Where is safety at home when my adults are not there?

My child care person is safety!

4. Where is safety at my friend's house?

My friend's grandma is safety!

5. Where is safety at the store?

The checkout person is safety!

6. Where is safety at the amusement park?

The ticket person is safety!

Checking First To Be Safe

Safety with animals, cars, people, matches, and electricity means checking first with your adults.

1. *Check First* with your adults before you play with animals unless you know them very well.

2. *Check First* with your adults before you get out of your car seat, unhook your seat belt, or get out of the car.

3. *Check First* with your adults before you go out the gate, out the door, or out of the house, even if something very interesting is happening.

4. Keep *Checking First* before you touch the stove, plug anything into an electric outlet, or use matches until your adults say it is safe.

 A publication of Kidpower Teenpower Fullpower International® www.kidpower.org For permission to copy, contact safety@kidpower.org

The Pizza Story

Even if you know someone well, Check First before you change your
plan about where you are going, who is with you, and what you are doing.

1. Chen and his sister are walking home after school.

2. Their dad drives up. He asks if they want pizza.

Hi kids! Let's get pizza!

Yeah, pizza!

3. Their mom is working at home. When her children don't come home after school, she gets worried. She tries to figure out where they are.

4. When their mom can't find her kids, she calls the police. They find the kids and their dad at the pizza parlor.

Hello, police. I am so worried. My kids aren't home, and I don't know where they are.

5. Mom is very glad and very mad.

WHY DIDN'T YOU CALL ME?!

We forgot. From now on, we will CHECK BEFORE WE CHANGE THE PLAN!

6. Their neighbor invites Chen and his sister to come over. They've been at his house before, but they remember to *check before they change their plans.*

Your mom says you can come over to my house for cookies.

We'd love to, but we need to Check First with Mom ourselves.

What's A Stranger?

A stranger is just someone you don't know well. Strangers can look like anybody. Most people are good, and most strangers are good.

1. You don't need to worry about strangers. You just need to Stay Together and Check First with your adults.

2. You will often meet lots of strangers on the first day of a school or of a class.

3. No matter what people are wearing or look like, they are still strangers unless you really know them.

4. People you know a little are called acquaintances. Until you know them well, Check First with your adults.

 A publication of Kidpower Teenpower Fullpower International® www.kidpower.org For permission to copy, contact safety@kidpower.org

Checking First Rules With Strangers

If you are on your own, go to your adult and Check First
before you take anything from, get close to, or talk to a stranger.

1. Before you take anything from a stranger, even if it is yours...

2. Check First!

3. Before you open the door...

4. Check First!

5. Before you get close to or talk with a stranger...

6. Check First!

More Times To Check First

Check First so your adults know who is with you, where you are going, and what you are doing, especially with people you don't know well.

1. If someone you don't know tries to take your photo...

You are so cute! Let me take your photo for our website.

2. Move Away and Check First!

Thank you for checking first. No, we don't want your photo on a website.

Can that lady take my photo for their website??

3. If someone else has an emergency. Check First!

My child is lost. Please look at this photo!

This is a stranger. I will get help by checking first.

4. If someone is wearing a uniform. Check First!

A kid is hurt. Come with me to help!

This is a stranger. I am going to CHECK FIRST and get my grown-ups to help!

 A publication of Kidpower Teenpower Fullpower International® www.kidpower.org For permission to copy, contact safety@kidpower.org

How Can A Stranger Know Your Name?

Even if someone looks familiar and knows your name, move away and check first with your adults, unless you are sure you really know this person.

1. If someone calls out your name at the park or in another public place, all the strangers nearby can learn your name.

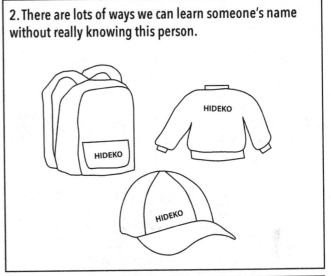

2. There are lots of ways we can learn someone's name without really knowing this person.

3. Hideko is playing in the hall by her apartment. A stranger calls her name.

4. The stranger is nice, but Hideko moves away.

5. Hideko Checks First.

6. Hideko's grown-up helps her.

A publication of Kidpower Teenpower Fullpower International® www.kidpower.org For permission to copy, contact safety@kidpower.org

Getting Help In Emergencies

If you have an **emergency** and cannot **Check First**, your
Safety Plan is to **Get Help** even from someone you don't know.

1. You can get help from paramedics.

2. You can get help from firefighters.

3. You can get help from a search party.

4. You can get help from a woman with children in an EMERGENCY.

 A publication of Kidpower Teenpower Fullpower International® www.kidpower.org For permission to copy, contact safety@kidpower.org

Your Safety Plan If You Are Lost In A Store

Remind your adults if they forget to agree on a safety plan with you about how to get help when you go out in public.

1. Everywhere you go, make a safety plan with your grown-up for what to do if you get lost.

2. The first thing to do if you are lost is stand tall and still like the trunk of a tree. Look around to see if you can find your grown-up.

3. The next thing to do is yell for your grown-up.

4. If that does not work, go to the front of the checkout line, not the back. Interrupt the cashier and ask for help.

5. If the cashier does not understand, ask again and say that you are lost.

6. To help your grown-up find you, you may need to tell the cashier your grown-up's name.

When To Wait And When To Interrupt

You might have to wait if you want something.
Interrupt and keep asking for help if there is a safety problem.

1. You *wait* when your mom is busy on the computer even if you want to talk to her.

2. You *interrupt* your mom when the pot is boiling over on the stove.

3. You *wait* when your Dad is on the phone even if he has been talking forever.

4. You *interrupt* your dad when a kid is hurting another kid.

5. You go to the end of the line and *wait* your turn when you want to buy something in a store.

6. You go to the front of the line and *interrupt* the cashier so you can get help if you are lost in the store.

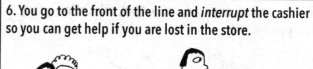

A publication of Kidpower Teenpower Fullpower International® www.kidpower.org For permission to copy, contact safety@kidpower.org

Yell, Leave, And Get Help If You Are Scared

You can use the power of your voice and body to get away and get to Safety.

1. A big kid pushes Jordan. He is scared.

2. Jordan yells, runs, and goes to his teacher for help.

3. A dog barks. Elise is scared.

4. Elise can tell the dog firmly to stop. She can back away and go to her mom for help.

5. Some kids are very angry. Jeremy is scared.

6. Jeremy yells, runs, and goes to the yard duty person for help.

The Big Kid Being Scary Story

If someone is acting unsafely, you can protect yourself by
yelling in a strong voice and running to your adult to get help.

1. Brittany likes to go to the store with her mom.

2. A big kid grabs Brittany, and she is scared.

3. Brittany pulls her arm away and yells.

NO!!

4. She uses her Stop Sign and a big voice to scare the big kid.

NO!

5. Brittany runs and yells for help.

I NEED HELP!!

6. Her mom helps her, and the big kid is sorry.

It's not funny to scare little kids.

I'm sorry.

 A publication of Kidpower Teenpower Fullpower International® www.kidpower.org For permission to copy, contact safety@kidpower.org

Introduction To Boundaries

A boundary is like a fence. It sets a limit. Personal boundaries
are the limits between people. Good personal boundaries help us to
have more fun and fewer problems with people we know.

The rules about personal boundaries are:

1. **We each belong to ourselves.** You belong to you, and I belong to me. This means that your body belongs to you—AND so does your personal space, your feelings, your time, your thoughts—ALL of you! This means that other people belong to themselves too.

2. **Some things are not a choice.** This is true for adults as well as kids. Especially for kids, touch for health and safety is often not a choice.

3. **Problems should not be secrets.** Anything that bothers you, me, or anybody else should not have to be a secret, even if telling makes someone upset or embarrassed. Also, presents, photos, videos, games, activities, and any kind of touch should not have to be a secret.

4. **Keep telling until you get help.** When you have a problem, find an adult you trust and keep on telling until you get the help you need.

1. We each belong to ourselves.

2. Some things are not a choice.

3. Problems should not be secrets.

4. Keep telling until you get help.

The Bath Story

This story shows how the boundary rules can work in real life.

1. Sometimes Indira does not want to take a bath.

2. Her mother says she has to because she is dirty.

3. Indira can tell everyone that she is angry that she had to have a bath.

4. Keep telling until you get help. The mom in this story did the right thing by saying the little girl could tell if she wanted to.

The safety rule is that kids should be able to talk with adults they trust about anything that bothers them.

But, suppose that this girl's mom had said, "Please don't tell! That would be too embarrassing."

If the mom had done this, she would have been making a safety mistake. Even though taking a bath was not the girl's choice, she should be able to talk about her feelings.

 A publication of Kidpower Teenpower Fullpower International® www.kidpower.org For permission to copy, contact safety@kidpower.org

The Trash Can For Hurting Words

If people say hurting words to you, you can protect your feelings.
Throw the hurting words away, and say something kind to yourself.

1. Sharona imagines catching hurtling words instead of letting them inside her body or her mind.

Go away, STUPID!

STUPID

2. Sharona throws the hurting words into the trash, and she puts kind words into her heart.

I am SMART!

STUPID

Trash

3. Sharona puts her hand on her hip. Imagine the hole it makes is her Kidpower Trash Can. She catches the hurting words, pushes them through her Trash Can, and says something nice to herself.

I'm smart!

STUPID

4. Louie uses his Kidpower Trash Can even with friends.

Weirdo!

I like myself!

WEIRD

5. Anna makes a Trash Can with her mind.

Useless!!

USELESS

I am IMPORTANT!

6. Heidi uses her Trash Can when she says something mean to herself.

I make such dumb mistakes!

Mistakes can help me learn!

DUMB MISTAKES

Taking In Compliments

Compliments are kind words that help you feel good about yourself. When someone gives you a compliment, take it inside your heart, and say, "Thank you!"

1. Latisha likes what her little sister built. Her little sister throws the compliment away.

2. Latisha tells her again. She wants her little sister to believe the compliment.

3. Kyle tells his older brother that he looks cool. His big brother throws the compliment away.

4. Kyle tries again because he wants his big brother to take good words into his heart, not throw them away.

 A publication of Kidpower Teenpower Fullpower International® www.kidpower.org For permission to copy, contact safety@kidpower.org

Choice And Not A Choice

Your body belongs to you, but some things are not a choice.

1. Going to bed is *not a choice.*

2. Getting a hug *should be a choice.*

3. Being stopped from hitting is *not a choice.*

4. Standing up on your own instead of being picked up *should be a choice.*

5. Opening your mouth at the dentist is *not a choice.*

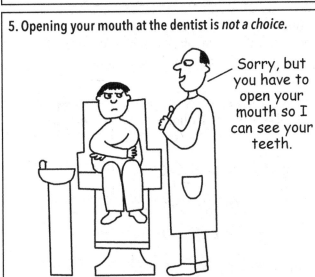

6. Having the dentist pat your head *should be a choice.*

Rules On Touch And Play For Fun And Affection

The safety rule is that touch and play for fun and affection should be the choice of each person, safe, allowed by the adults in charge, and not a secret.

1. Touch and play for fun and affection should be the *choice of each person*. In this example both people and animals like this touch, so it is okay.

2. One person wants to tickle and the other wants to stop. So it is not okay to keep tickling.

Tickle tickle!

Stop that game. I don't like it!

3. Touch and play for fun and affection should be *safe*. Miguel is being gentle and safe, so it is okay for him to hold the baby.

4. Miguel and the baby are having fun, but holding a baby like this is *not* being safe. This touch is not okay because someone could get hurt.

Be careful! That is NOT safe!

5. Touch and play for fun and affection should be *okay with the grown-ups in charge*. The boy is helping the girl clean her face. This follows the rules of their house.

Thank you for wiping her face.

6. This touch is *not* okay even though both kids are having fun and being safe. It is against the rules of the grown-ups in this house to play with food.

NO playing with FOOD! That is NOT allowed!

 A publication of Kidpower Teenpower Fullpower International® www.kidpower.org For permission to copy, contact safety@kidpower.org

The Sloppy Kisses Story

There are lots of ways to show you care about someone—like waving, shaking hands, making a drawing, saying something kind, or giving a high-five.

1. Marcel likes to give his big sister sloppy kisses.

2. Sometimes she does not like it. This means Marcel has to stop even if he still wants to give her kisses.

3. Marcel's sister can love him, and he can love her—and she can still tell him to stop.

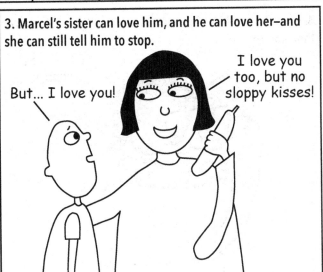

4. Kisses have to be okay with each person.

5. Now they are both happy.

6. When Marcel's aunt comes to visit, he can tell her what kinds of kiss he wants. Kisses have to be the choice of each person.

Safety With Touch Means You Can Always Tell

Some kinds of touch are not your choice—and sometimes
you change your mind. Any kind of touch should not be a secret.

1. Touch for health and safety is not a choice.

2. Problems with touch or anything else should not be secrets.

3. If something bothers you, you can tell all your grown-ups.

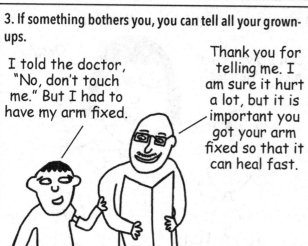

4. If Iris likes to kiss her Grandpa and he likes it too, this is their choice.

5. Iris can always change her mind.

6. Iris can always tell what happened.

 A publication of Kidpower Teenpower Fullpower International® www.kidpower.org For permission to copy, contact safety@kidpower.org

The Sleepover Story

Anytime you have a problem, even if you need to wake
up a grown-up in the middle of the night, your job is to get help.

1. Simon likes to go to his cousin's house for a sleepover. They jump on the bed and laugh.

2. It gets dark and a little scary. They like cuddling together to feel safe.

3. Simon's cousin starts to crowd over to his side of the bed. Simon moves away so much that he falls out of bed.

4. Simon goes to get help from his aunt even though it is the middle of the night.

5. Simon's aunt just wants him to go back to bed. He keeps telling her until she understands and helps him.

I can't sleep.

What are you doing up? Go back to bed.

6. Simon's aunt makes a bed for him on the couch so he can be comfortable.

Thanks, Auntie.

Sleep well.

How To Stop Unwanted Touch

Your body belongs to you. You can tell people to stop if you do not like touch or games like kisses, hugs, roughhousing, tickling, or jokes.

1. If Kim likes it when her friend tickles her, that is fine.

2. Kim can change her mind. She uses her eyes, words, and body to tell her friend when she wants him to stop.

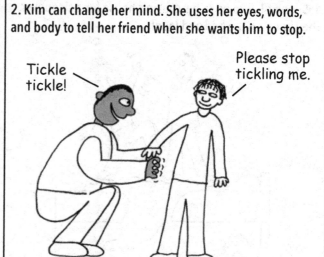

3. If he does not listen, she can stand up, move away, make a fence with her hands, and say stop.

4. If her friend is sad or mad because Kim told him to stop, she tells him that she is sorry but he still has to stop.

5. If Kim's friend tries to give her a treat so she will let him keep tickling, this is an unsafe bribe.

6. Even if Kim has to promise not to tell, the safety rule is to go *tell* and keeping telling until she gets help.

 A publication of Kidpower Teenpower Fullpower International® www.kidpower.org For permission to copy, contact safety@kidpower.org

Fun Surprises And Unsafe Secrets

Fun surprises are safe because most people know, and they do not break your safety rules. Secrets about presents or treats someone gives you are NOT safe.

1. A surprise party or present for someone is a good secret that the person being surprised will know about soon.

2. People who ask you to keep treats or gifts a secret are making a safety mistake.

3. Most grown-ups who care about you will understand.

4. Even if your grown-ups might be annoyed, it is still important to tell.

What Is A Bribe?

Safe bribes are okay for everyone to know about and
are NOT used to try to get you to break your safety rules.

---

1. A bribe is like a trade. A safe bribe has to be okay with both people.

If you will let me play with your puzzle, I'll let you use my special pens.

No, thanks. I want to finish my puzzle.

---

2. A safe bribe is one that everyone knows about.

If you clean up quickly, I'll let you stay outside longer.

---

3. A bribe is NOT safe when it is secret or tries to get you to do something against your safety rules.

If you let me keep tickling you, I'll sneak you some more cake!

---

4. If someone tries to give you an unsafe bribe, say, "Stop or I'll tell—and tell a grown-up you trust even if the person stops.

OOPS!

Sorry!

Stop or I'll tell!

 A publication of Kidpower Teenpower Fullpower International® www.kidpower.org For permission to copy, contact safety@kidpower.org

The Safety Rules About Private Areas

It is important to understand what is safe—and
what is not safe—about people and their private areas.

1. Private areas are the parts of the body that can be covered by a bathing suit.

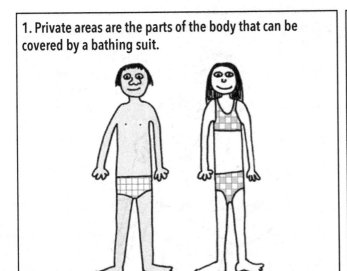

2. For play or teasing, other people should not touch your private areas. They should not ask you to touch their private areas either.

Let's take off our clothes so we can play doctor!

That is against our safety rules. We can play doctor with our clothes on.

3. Sometimes grown-ups have to touch kids' private areas to help them.

I need to put medicine on your sore.

4. Touch of any kind should never EVER be a secret. You should always be able to talk about things you don't like.

Mom put medicine on my bottom today! I did not like it.

Thank you for telling me. I am sorry you didn't like it.

5. The safety rule is that people should not show kids pictures or videos about people and their private areas for fun, and it should never be a secret even if for health.

Look at these pictures of grown-ups.

They don't have clothes on. Stop or I'll tell.

6. Even if the person stops, you should tell about anything that bothers you.

Thank you for telling me. We will help him understand about the safety rules.

My friend's brother tried to show me pictures on his computer of people touching their private areas. I said, "Stop or I will tell."

The Keep Telling Until You Get Help Story

Sometimes you have to be persistent and keep asking until you get the help you need. Remember that it is never too late to tell.

1. Today kids at school locked Irina in the bathroom. She was scared.

2. Irina tells her dog. He listens but he cannot help her.

3. Irina tells her mom. She is too busy to understand.

4. Irina tells her grandpa. He listens but not for very long.

5. The safety rule is to tell a grown-up you trust when you have problems and to keep telling until someone helps.

6. Irina's teacher listens. She understands and helps her.

 A publication of Kidpower Teenpower Fullpower International® www.kidpower.org For permission to copy, contact safety@kidpower.org

The Busy Mom Story

Adults cannot read your mind, and they sometimes don't understand. You might need to explain, "This is about my safety!"

1. Alex has a safety problem. He feels bad.

LOSER!

2. His Mom is talking to her friend.

Blah blah blah very busy blah

blah blah blah

3. Alex asks his Mom for help, but she is too busy.

I'm busy!

I need help!

4. Alex tries again a little later.

OH!

But Mom, this is about my safety!

5. Alex's Mom listens. He feels better.

What happened?

A kid at school made me feel bad!

6. They make a plan to help Alex be safe.

I'm glad you told me! We will figure out what to do.

A publication of Kidpower Teenpower Fullpower International® www.kidpower.org For permission to copy, contact safety@kidpower.org

The Tired Grandpa Story

Even if your grown-ups are tired, grumpy, or busy, they care about your safety!

1. Sheri is sad because she is getting teased about her wheelchair.

2. She needs help, but her Grandpa is asleep.

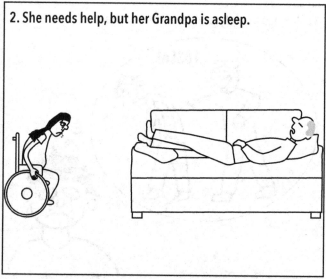

3. Sheri wakes her Grandpa up, but he is tired.

4. Sheri persists because she is hurting inside.

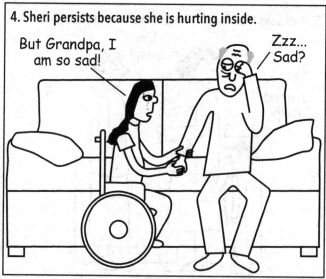

5. Her Grandpa listens because Sheri's safety is important.

6. Her Grandpa helps Sheri feel better, and they will make a safety plan to stop kids from teasing her.

 A publication of Kidpower Teenpower Fullpower International® www.kidpower.org For permission to copy, contact safety@kidpower.org

People Safety Skills To Stop Bullying

Use your awareness, move out of reach, protect your feelings, and speak up to take charge of your safety when kids try to hurt you, scare you, or make you feel bad.

---

1. If someone tries to bully you by being scary, you can use your Walk Away Power, and get help. Being mean back will make the problem bigger, not better.

2. If someone tries to bully you by saying rude things, you can throw the hurting words in your Trash Can, and say something kind to yourself.

---

3. If someone tries to bully you by taking your turn, you can say, "NO! Please wait!"

4. If someone tries to bully you by tripping or pushing, you can use your awareness to notice what this person is trying to do, and then Move Out of Reach.

More Ways To Stop Bullying

You have the right to be safe and respected everywhere you go—and the responsibility to act safely and respectfully towards others.

1. If friends try to bully you by telling you not to play with someone else, you do not have to do what they say.

2. If someone tries to bully you by not letting you join the game, you can keep asking. If you see this happen to someone else, you can speak up, or get help.

3. If some kids try to bully you by leaving you out, you can protect your feelings, and find someone else to be your friend!

4. You have the right to be safe with your feelings and your body. If you need help to stop bullying problems, you can ask the adults in charge for help.

 A publication of Kidpower Teenpower Fullpower International® www.kidpower.org For permission to copy, contact safety@kidpower.org

Tattling And Telling—What's The Difference?

Tattling is when you are telling on kids just to get them into trouble.
Telling to get help is when you are asking for help to solve a problem with someone.

1. Don't tell on kids just because they are not doing what you think they should.

2. Unless there is a safety problem, stay in charge of what YOU are doing instead of what other kids are doing.

3. Telling to get help is NOT tattling or being a tattletale.

4. Sometimes grown-ups get confused about the difference between "tattling" and "telling to get help."

5. You might need to persist in getting help.

6. Tell your grown-ups any time you have a safety problem.

Safety With Cars

Use your awareness, stay together, and check first!

1. Not Safe
Running into the street is not safe because you might get hit by a car.

2. Safe
Your safety rule is to **stop, look, and wait** for your grown-up.

3. Not Safe
Even if you are with a grown-up, it is not safe to walk in front of a car until it has stopped all the way.

4. Safe
Your safety rule is to **look** and **wait** until the street is clear or until the cars are all stopped.

5. Not Safe
When a car backs up in a driveway, the driver cannot see a kid on a bike. It is not safe to go or ride your bike behind a backing up car.

BE CAREFUL!!

6. Safe
Wait until the car is done backing up before you cross the driveway.

7. Not Safe
It is not safe to walk away from your grown-up when you get out of your car.

8. Safe
Your safety rule is to stay next to your grown-up when you are outside your car.

A publication of Kidpower Teenpower Fullpower International® www.kidpower.org For permission to copy, contact safety@kidpower.org

The Big Sister Story

Dedicated to the big sisters and big brothers everywhere who use their power to help keep their younger brothers and sisters safe!

1. Zara's little brother wants to go out the door. She holds the door closed.

2. Zara's little brother tries to climb out the window. She grabs him and yells for help.

3. Zara's little brother tries to get out of his car seat while they are driving. Zara yells for help.

4. Zara's little brother tries to climb over the wall and into the water with the ducks. Zara grabs him and yells for help. Her little brother is annoyed. Her parents thank her for stopping him from falling into the pond, while still staying safe herself.

A publication of Kidpower Teenpower Fullpower International® www.kidpower.org For permission to copy, contact safety@kidpower.org

kidpower® Safety Signals for Everyone, Everywhere To Help Prevent And Solve Problems

Safety Signals are simple gestures, drawings, and words to help all of us remember important People Safety ideas and skills.

Wait Power
Hold your own hands to show times when you need to wait patiently to stay safe and be respectful.

Stay Aware Power
Point towards your eyes, turn your head, and look around to signal how to pay attention and act alert.

Stay Together Power
Start with your palms apart and facing outwards, and then move them together to signal staying together to stay safe out in public.

Check First Power
Clasp your forearm with the other hand to show checking first with the adults who care about you before you change your plan.

Think First Power
Pat your head gently to show thinking first about what to do when the unexpected happens or someone is acting unsafely.

Walk Away Power
Use your fingers like legs and walk them on your arm to help you remember to walk away from any person or situation that might be unsafe.

Roll Away Power
Roll your fingers along the other arm to show using wheels to roll away from trouble and get to safety.

Get Help Power
Put your arms in front of you with palms facing up like a bridge to show reaching out to get help or to make a connection.

The full set of Kidpower Safety Signals can be downloaded from our online Library at www.kidpower.org

 A publication of Kidpower Teenpower Fullpower International® www.kidpower.org For permission to copy, contact safety@kidpower.org

kidpower Safety Signals For Taking Charge Of Our Feelings, Words, And Bodies

The keys to remembering to use People Safety strategies and skills in real life are simplicity, repetition, consistency, fun, and practice.

Calm Down Power

Press your palms together, straighten your back, breathe deeply and slowly, and feel your feet to calm down.

Mouth Closed Power

Squeeze your lips together to stop yourself from doing anything unsafe with what you say or do with your mouth.

Hands And Feet Down Power

Imagine you are about to bother or hurt someone with your hands or feet and then pull them down to your sides or the floor.

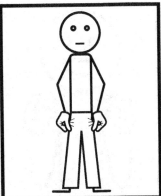

Hang On Power

To show stopping yourself from touching or hitting someone, hang onto your sides or pockets.

Speak Up Power

Put your hand in front of your mouth and move it outwards to show speaking up about what you do and do not want.

Fence Power

Put your arms in front of you waist-high with palms facing downwards to show making a fence to set boundaries with someone who is bothering you.

Trash Can Power

Put a hand on your hip and pretend the hole it makes is your personal trash can. Use your other hand to catch hurting words and throw them away.

Heart Power

Reach forward and then press your hands into your chest to show scooping kind words into your heart, protecting your heart, and using your heart to be kind to others.

The full set of Kidpower Safety Signals can be downloaded from our online Library at www.kidpower.org

A publication of Kidpower Teenpower Fullpower International® www.kidpower.org For permission to copy, contact safety@kidpower.org

kidpower® Safety Signals For Healthy Boundaries With People We Know

These Safety Signals help everyone, everywhere remember the boundary rules and principles for staying safe and having fun with people we know.

Safety Signals about the four Kidpower Boundary Rules.

We each belong to ourselves
Point to yourself, sit tall, and smile to show that each person's body, time, feelings, and thoughts are important.

Some things are not a choice
Shrug and smile to show that some things are required, and boundaries often have to be negotiated, even for adults.

Problems should not be secrets
Hold a finger in front of your lips. Now move the finger away from your mouth to show that we are safer when we can talk about our problems.

Keep telling until you get help
Pretend that your hands are talking to each other. One hand asks, "I need help." The other hand replies, "I will help you."

Safety Signals for the Kidpower Safety Rule that "Touch, play, or games for fun or affection should be safe, the choice of each person, allowed by the adults in charge, and not a secret, which means that others can know."

Safe
Hug yourself to show that we all deserve to be and feel safe.

The choice of each person
Put two thumbs up to show that each person needs to agree about touch or games for fun or affection.

Allowed by the adults in charge
Curl up your fingers and move your hand up and down to show the head of the adult in charge nodding in approval.

Others Can Know
Raise both arms above your head with your palms facing up to show that touch, play, and affection should NOT be a secret.

The full set of Kidpower Safety Signals can be downloaded from our online Library at www.kidpower.org

A publication of Kidpower Teenpower Fullpower International® www.kidpower.org For permission to copy, contact safety@kidpower.org

Discussions And Practices
To Build Understanding And Skills

Here is how to make discussing, practicing, and using these skills successful.

1. The more that everyone in a family, school, or youth group has a common understanding about safety, the safer they are. For this reason, we recommend that you read the stories together, act out what the people are doing in the drawings, and discuss how these ideas might work in your daily lives.

2. We will be safer and have better relationships if we keep using these skills in everyday life. Coach kids to be successful in avoiding and solving problems with people—in the same way that you might learn to be safe with water, food, fire, cars, and bikes—at home, in your neighborhood, in nature, at school, at work, and in your community.

3. Don't let discomfort get in the way of safety. Review the Safety Plans and the People Safety skills in this book with children on a regular basis. Give special attention to actions that might be hard due to embarrassment, such as interrupting busy adults when you have a problem, yelling to get help, or speaking up if someone is bullying. Remember that feeling embarrassed, upset, or shy is normal, but it is important not to let these emotions stop us from getting help or making the safest choices.

4. Stay relevant by adapting these examples and practices to make sense for each person's age, life situation, and abilities. Tell younger children or kids who think very literally, "I am just pretending so we can practice!" If necessary, simplify the information by using fewer words, or change the wording to ensure understanding. You can also expand on the concepts presented by discussing with young people how to adapt these skills and ideas to handle more complicated situations.

5. Instead of testing or tricking children, coach them to be successful. When you are practicing, pause to give kids a chance to try to use the skill. If they get stuck, coach them in exactly what to say, how to say it, and what to do with their bodies, as if you were the director or a prompter in a play. Encourage children to project an assertive attitude of both power and respect in their body language, choice of words, and posture, rather than acting either passively or aggressively.

6. Make the practices fun by being positive and calm rather than anxious. Reward small steps with encouragement, remembering that mistakes are part of learning. Celebrate progress rather than looking for perfection.

7. Keep the focus on how to stay safe rather than on the bad things that can happen. Going into detail about the ways we can get hurt just makes kids anxious without making them safer. Worrying and talking about safety problems can feel as if we are doing something—but are not nearly as effective as actually having a clear plan and practicing how to implement it so that we are prepared to take action.

8. Give discussing, practicing, and using these skills the same priority that you give other issues related to health and safety. These are crucial skills that can prevent problems and make daily life safer and more fun. If you encounter resistance, acknowledge that it is normal to not want to practice and to feel as if we already know what do so. However, rehearsing how to handle different kinds of problems is for our safety and must be a high priority. Discussing is not the same as actually practicing. Even if they express lots of resistance, most children also enjoy showing that they know what to do.

Kidpower Protection Promise (page 9)

Discuss this message often with all children in your life, making it relevant for their situations. Remind yourself to be a safe person for kids to come to by really listening with compassion even if a concern does not seem important to you or seems like the child's fault, without lecturing, scolding, or joking.

Directions for discussion and practices

Be aware, calm, respectful, and confident (page 10)

Explain that "People bother you less and listen to you more if you are aware, calm, respectful, and confident." Discuss what these words mean.

To practice, coach children to stand or sit tall and turn their heads to look around. Walk behind them and do something silly for them to look at. Ask them to tell you what they saw so you know they are really looking around. Next, let children start close to you and walk towards another spot a little ways from you, glancing back to see what you are doing and then looking where they are going. Again, do something silly for them to report when they get to their spot.

Use different kinds of power and move out of reach (pages 11 to 13)

We want children to know that there are many ways to be powerful. Coach children to squeeze their lips together to use Mouth Closed Power. Coach children to raise their hands as if to hit or touch something they shouldn't and instead pull their hands down to their sides to use Hands Down Power. Coach children to put their hands in front of themselves like a wall and say, "Stop!" to use Stop Power.

Pretend to be another kid who is starting to get mad, or who is about to throw things or shove on the playground or in line. Coach children to use their Walk Away Power to move out of reach. With an individual child, you can come up with even more ideas of different ways to be powerful.

Use the coaching guide on the bottom of page 12 to practice Moving Out Of Reach. Start close together and have kids practice backing away. You can then act out the Leaving Story and the Walk Away Power Story by pretending to be a grumpy kid and having kids practice moving away from you with awareness, calm, and respectful confidence.

Check First to be safe (pages 14 to 17)

Unless children are independent enough to be somewhere or do something without an adult supervising their safety, their best strategy of self-protection is almost always to Check First with their adults before they change their plan about what they are doing, who is with them, and where they are going - including with people they know.

Practice the Check First rule using relevant examples from a child's life, such as: before you open the door, before you use the stove, before you get close to an animal at the park (you can use a toy animal to pretend), before you pick up something sharp, before going with a friendly neighbor even if this is a kid who invites you to do something fun, and before you get close to someone you don't know well. Coach children to stand up, move away, and go to their adults to Check First. Now say, "Your Mom says you are supposed to come to my house." Coach kids walk away as they say, "I need to Check First myself!"

Know how to be safe with strangers (pages 18 to 21)

During your daily life, point out people who are strangers and people who children know well. Discuss that a stranger can know your name or wear a uniform. Remind kids that most people are good, and that most strangers are good. However, if you don't know someone well, you Check First before you talk with, get close to, or take anything from someone you don't know well.

To practice, pretend to be a stranger. Approach the child calling the child's name or holding something that belongs to the child. Coach the child to stand up, move away, and go to his or her adult to Check First. You can have another adult or child or even a toy pretending to be this child's grown-up. Have this person say, "Thank you for checking first!"

While you are pretending to be the "stranger," act like someone who just doesn't know the safety rules rather than being scary. Coach kids to be successful in standing up and moving away rather than getting too close to them. Reinforce keeping a distance from people the child doesn't know well by staying far away from him or her when you are practicing Stranger Safety skills.

Know your Safety Plan if you are having an emergency or are lost (pages 22 to 24)

Children need to know the exceptions to the Check First rules. Make and review your family's Safety Plan for getting help each time your child goes to a new place. Pretend you are about to go into a store or park, and coach children to ask, "What's our safety plan if we get lost?" Any plan that uses a mobile phone should also have a backup plan in case this doesn't work.

Encourage children to buy something from the cashier so that they know how to interact with this person. Take children to the place you want them to go if they are lost or bothered in a store or out in public. Make sure they can find this place if they need help. If children cannot follow their Safety Plan, discuss backup plans for getting help that make sense for that situation, such as asking a woman with children, calling police, etc. Unless they are having a big emergency, children should not leave the place you were planning for them to be.

Tell children, "The rules are different in emergencies. You might need to get help from people you don't know if you are hurt, someone is making you feel scared, or you are lost in nature. You might need to go to a safer place to get away from a fire or other big safety emergency."

Getting help in public can be embarrassing. Pretend to be a busy, impatient cashier, and coach children to come to the front of the line, interrupt you, and be persistent in asking for help because they are being bothered by someone, their friend is hurt, or they are lost.

Practice with children yelling for help as if they have hurt their leg and can't move. If they are lost in nature where there are no stores, coach them to stay where they are if it is safe to do so and to call for help—and perhaps to hug a tree—and to accept help from a ranger or other stranger such as a woman with children or a person calling their name.

Yell, leave, and get help if you are scared (page 25)
Pretend to be someone acting a little unsafe (not in a frightening way). Say something like, "Hey kid, get over here!" Avoid speaking or acting in ways that might put scary or upsetting images into a child's mind. Do not pretend to grab children.

Remember success-based learning—coach kids to set a firm boundary and to use a strong yelling voice. Coach children to put their hands in front of their chests with their arms bent and palms facing out to make a wall and yell, "STOP!" As the pretend Scary Person, act startled and stop. Coach children to run to Safety, yelling "I NEED HELP!" Coach someone pretending to be the Safety adult say, "I will help you."

Big kid being scary, practicing the arm grab escape (page 26)
Practice the arm grab escape with children one at a time by grabbing one of their arms gently but firmly. When practicing, you are holding your child's arms hard enough so they feel a little trapped, but not so hard that you bruise them, injure them, or make it impossible for them to escape. The goal is for them to learn the technique.

Have the child standing up in front of you and grab their arm making sure there is enough room around you so you do not bump into things when practicing. Keep in mind that the child will be pulling away from you so they need more space behind them. Coach them to clasp their hands together (make sure they are not intertwining their fingers) and use the leverage of their arm by turning and moving their body away and keeping their arm close to their body. When practicing, they should loudly "NO" when they pull away—and then also practice going to safety.

The first time you practice, let go as soon as you feel the child pull away. Kids can pull away with a lot of force so be prepared and make sure they are also in balance and prepared to catch themselves when they pull away. Then let the child practice again and hold on a little tighter. Coach children to pull their hands out against the place where your fingertips come together with your thumb, because this spot is the weakest part of someone's grip. Coach them to yell, "NO!" and "HELP!" loudly while pulling away.

Protect your feelings from hurting words and taking in compliments (page 29 to 30)
Children are emotionally safest if they can take in the kind things people say to them or they say to themselves and protect themselves from the hurting words. To practice, coach children to pretend to catch hurting words in the air, throw them into a real trash can or a trash can they make with their bodies, and say something nice to themselves.

Put a hand on your hip and show that the hole makes a personal Trash Can. Practice together—for example, if someone says, "You are stupid," children can catch the word "STUPID," throw it in their personal Trash Can and say, "I am SMART!"

Make sure children know that you are just pretending so they can practice and that you do not mean the words you are saying. Do not have children practice saying hurtful words—you want them to focus on the skill of protecting their feelings.

Give children meaningful compliments for them to take into their hearts while saying, "Thank you!" Have them practice giving compliments to each other—and to you!

The rule is that touch and games for fun or affection have to be okay with each person, safe, allowed by the adults in charge, and NOT a secret (page 32)

Play the "Asking for a hug"" game by having children ask you, "May I have a hug?" Say, "No thanks. No hugs today. We can wave." And wave. Then reverse roles and ask, "May I have a hug?" Coach children to say, "No thanks. No hugs today. Just wave." And wave. This practice lets children rehearse setting and accepting boundaries on unwanted touch for affection.

Practice saying yes or no to touch and games by having kids take turns saying, "Let's _____, (play tag, wrestle, have a race, or play catch)!" Coach them both to give and respect different responses. For example, "That's great!" Or, "No thanks!" Or, "We'll have to go outside because we might break things inside." Or, "Not in the street!" Or, "Not at the dinner table!"

Stop unwanted touch or teasing (page 36)

These skills prepare children to persist in setting boundaries if someone doesn't notice, doesn't listen, tries to make them feel wrong by using emotional coercion, offers a bribe, or makes them promise not to tell. Teach children to use their voices, bodies, and words to set clear boundaries with people they know, such as family, friends, and peers.

To practice, touch children on the shoulder and ask, "Do you like this? If you like this touch, it is fine. But can you change your mind? Yes, you can. Now, pretend you don't like this touch any more." Coach children to give you back your hand in a firm, polite way and say, in a clear, respectful voice, "Please stop." Pretend not to listen; put your hand back. Coach children to stand or move back, make a fence with their hands, look at you and say in a calm, firm voice, and say in a powerful and respectful way, "I said, 'Please stop!' I don't like it."

Next, pretend to be sad or annoyed so children can practice dealing with emotional coercion. Say, "But I like you. I thought you were my friend." Coach children to project an assertive attitude while they say, "I don't mean to hurt your feelings and I am your friend, and I still want you to stop." Or just, "Sorry and stop!"

Discuss when bribes are safe or unsafe. Practice resisting unsafe bribes. Say, "I'll give you a treat (offer something you think the child you are practicing with would like) if you let me touch your shoulder after you asked me to stop. But don't tell anybody, okay?" Coach each child to say, "Stop or I'll tell!" You can coach them to add, "I don't keep touch or gifts a secret."

For children who can understand (normally children over 5 or 6 years old), give them the chance to practice promising not to tell even though they are going to tell an adult they trust as soon as they can. Pretend to get angry or upset without acting intensely or making specific threats. Say, "Promise not to tell anyone or something bad will happen!" Or, "You have to promise not to tell or I won't be able to play with you anymore." Or, "Please don't tell, or I could get into trouble."

Coach children to say, "I won't tell if you stop." Explain that,"Most of the time we want you to tell the truth and keep your promises. But you can lie and break a promise to stay safe, as long as you get away as soon as you can and tell an adult you trust and keep telling until someone does something about it."

Know the difference between safe and unsafe secrets (Page 37)

Very young children should just be taught not to keep anything a secret. As they get older, discuss the difference between a surprise party or gift that everyone knows about except the person being surprised (who will find out) and a secret that breaks your safety rules that most people will NOT know about.

Know the difference between safe and unsafe bribes (page 38)
Discuss the difference between rewards that you get for doing something helpful or good for you and bribes to get you to do something against your safety rules and that might hurt you or someone else.

Safety rules about private areas (page 39)
Discuss your family's rules about private areas with your child in a calm and matter-of-fact way. Make sure to review this page with your child and review your safety rules about private areas about every six months.

Go and get help when you have a problem and keep trying until you get help (pages 40 to 42)
Remind children that touch, games, presents, money, activities, photos, videos, and problems should not be secrets. Discuss different safety problems children might have and who to ask for help if they need it. Tell children to pretend to have a safety problem. Pretend to be a busy adult (act as if you are reading a book, watching TV, or working). Coach children to interrupt you to ask for help. Say, "I'm busy."

Coach children to ask again. Say, "Don't bother me." Coach children to say, "This is about my safety." Listen, coaching children to tell the whole story. Say, "Thank you for telling me." If children do this well, do the practice again but be unsupportive by saying, "That's your problem. Go away." Coach children to find another adult to tell. Tell children, "Remember that it is not your fault if you have a problem even if you made a mistake and that it is never too late to tell."

Know what bullying is and how to stop it (pages 43 to 44)
Point out examples of bullying as they happen in real life, in stories, or in movies such as shunning, name-calling, intimidation, etc. Pretend to act like someone who is bullying by saying something mean. Coach the child to use her or his Trash Can and move away. Or coach the child to say, "Stop," and then leave to get help.

Coach kids in how to ask confidently and positively to be included and how to persist if excluded at first. Start by coaching the child to say, "I want to play." Or, "I want to join you." Pretend to reject the child by frowning and saying, "Go away. You're not good enough." Or, "There's too many already." Have the child throw away the hurting words and say, "I'm great." Coach the child to practice persisting instead of getting upset or giving up by saying in a cheerful and confident way, "I'll do my best." Or, "I'll get better if I practice." Or, "There's always room for one more." Or, "Give me a chance." Or, "The rule at school is everybody gets to play." Coach a child who is being left out to go find another child and invite that child to play.

Give a more verbal child the chance to practice being an advocate. Pretend to be unkind to someone else. Coach the child to say, "Stop. That is not kind!" Pretend to exclude another person so that the child can practice speaking up for someone else by saying, "Let her play!" Or, "Give him a chance!"

Pretend to be another child who is acting unsafely. Push the child gently and say something like, "Get over here, you dummy!" Coach the child to take a breath, throw the mean words away, use Mouth Closed Power by not answering back, and Walk Away Power by standing tall and leaving with awareness. Remind the child to go to an adult and get help because problems should not be secrets.

Know the difference between tattling and telling to get help (page 45)
Too often, kids don't talk about safety problems because they have been told not to "tattle" or be a "tattletale." Try not to use these labels. Instead, encourage kids to focus on their own responsibilities unless another kids is doing something that is unsafe—and to always talk about safety problems, even if someone will be annoyed with them.

Kidpower Safety Signals (pages 48 to 49)
Use these simple gestures, words, and drawings to review and help kids and adults remember core People Safety strategies and skills. Visit the Kidpower.org website for the full set.

Kidpower Services For All Ages And Abilities

Overview

Kidpower Teenpower Fullpower International is a global nonprofit leader dedicated to providing effective and empowering child protection, positive communication, and personal safety skills for all ages and abilities. Since 1989, Kidpower has served over 3 million children, teenagers, and adults, including those with difficult life challenges, locally and around the world through our in-person workshops, educational resources, and partnerships. We give our students the opportunity for successful practice of "People Safety" skills in ways that helps prepare them to develop healthy relationships, increase their confidence, take charge of their emotional and physical safety, and act safely and respectfully towards others. For more information, visit www.kidpower.org or contact safety@kidpower.org.

Workshops

Through our centers and traveling instructors, Kidpower has led workshops in over 60 countries spanning six continents. Our programs include: Parent/Caregiver seminars; Parent-Child workshops; training for educators and other professionals; classroom workshops; Family workshops; Teenpower self-defense workshops for teens; Collegepower for young people leaving home; Fullpower self-defense and boundary-setting workshops for adults; Seniorpower for older people; adapted programs for people with special needs; and workplace safety, communication, and team-building seminars. Our three-day Child Protection Advocates Training Institute prepares educators and other professionals, as well as parents and other caring adults, to use Kidpower's intervention, advocacy, and personal safety skills in their personal and professional lives.

Online Library

Our extensive online Library provides over 100 free People Safety resources including articles, videos, webinars, blogs, and podcasts. Free downloads of online publications like our Kidpower Safety Signals, coloring book, and handouts are available for individual use. We provide licensing for use of materials or content for charitable and educational purposes.

Books

We publish an extensive preschool through high school curriculum, as well as books about personal safety for adults, including: *The Kidpower Book for Caring Adults: Personal Safety, Self-Protection, Confidence, and Advocacy for Young People*; cartoon-illustrated *Safety Comics* and *Teaching Books* for children, teens, and adults; *Bullying: What Adults Need to Know and Do to Keep Kids Safe*; *Fullpower Relationship Safety Skills Handbook for Teens and Adults*; *One Strong Move: Cartoon-Illustrated Self-Defense Lessons*; *Earliest Teachable Moment: Personal Safety for Babies, Toddlers, and Preschoolers*; and *Face Bullying with Confidence: Creating Cultures of Respect and Safety for All Ages and Stages of Life*. Please visit our website bookstore for a complete list.

Coaching, Consulting, and Curriculum Development

Long-distance coaching by video-conferencing, telephone, and e-mail enables us to make our services accessible worldwide. We consult with a wide range of experts, organizations, and schools on how best to adapt our program to meet unserved needs and develop new curriculum to increase the People Safety knowledge for different people facing difficult life challenges.

Instructor Training and Center Development

Our very comprehensive certified instructor training program prepares qualified people to teach our programs and to establish centers and offices for organizing services in their communities under our organizational umbrella.

Acknowledgments

Kidpower is a tapestry of many different threads woven by many different hands. Our curriculum has grown from the ideas, questions, teaching, feedback, and stories of countless people since I first started working on child protection, personal safety, and self-defense issues in 1985.

I want to express my appreciation to each of our Kidpower instructors, board members, honorary trustees, senior program leaders, center directors, workshop organizers, advisors, volunteers, donors, parents, students, funding partners, service partners, family members, advocates, hosts, and office staff.

Thank you for the thought, care, time, and generosity that you have given to bring Kidpower Teenpower Fullpower International to where we are today. I feel honored to have you as colleagues and as friends.

Writing each person's story would be a book unto itself. You can learn about the remarkable people who have built and keep building our organization by reading *A Tapestry Woven By Many Different Hands* on our website.

I want to give special acknowledgement to people who have helped to create our cartoon-illustrated Safety Comics and Teaching Books series in many different ways.

Amanda Golert is a Senior Program Leader, Training and Curriculum Consultant, and our Sweden Center Director since 1999. Amanda's role has been crucial in the development of all of our cartoon-illustrated books as the artist, designer, and primary editor.

Timothy Dunphy, our Program Co-Founder, worked with me for many years to create our curriculum and still teaches and serves as a member of our training team.

Senior Program Leader **Chantal Keeney** provided major help with editing, teaching instructions, and content development of our original cartoon-illustrated curriculum.

Our California Program Director **Erika Leonard**; Montreal Center Director **Marylaine Léger**; New Zealand Center Co-Director **Cornelia Baumgartner**; Colorado Center Director **Jan Isaacs Henry**; and Chicago Center Director **Joe Connelly**, who also are all Senior Program Leaders, have each contributed important ideas and improvements to these Kidpower social stories, explanations, and skills over the years.

Finally, thank you to Kidpower Instructor and Senior Program Leader **John Luna-Sparks**, LCSW, CMP, for many years of support, including working with me to create our original Safety Signals.

About The Author

Irene van der Zande is the Founder and Executive Director of Kidpower Teenpower Fullpower International, a global non-profit leader dedicated to protecting people of all ages and abilities from bullying, violence, and abuse by empowering them with knowledge and skills.

Since 1989, Kidpower has served over 3 million children, teenagers, and adults, including those with special needs, through its positive and practical workshops, extensive free online Library, and publications.

Since Kidpower began, Irene has led the development of programs, training of instructors, and establishment of centers, working with a wide range of international experts in education, public safety, violence prevention, mental health, and the martial arts.

Irene has authored numerous books and articles in the child development, child protection, positive communication, and violence and abuse prevention and intervention fields, including the following:

The Parent/Toddler Group: A Model of Effective Intervention to Facilitate Normal Growth and Development, which is published by Cedars-Sinai Medical Center and used as a textbook for mental health and child education professionals; *1, 2, 3... The Toddler Years: A Guide for Parents and Caregivers*, which is used as a textbook in early childhood development programs in many colleges and has a foreword by early childhood development and Respect for Infant Educarers founder Magda Gerber; *The Kidpower Book for Caring Adults*, a comprehensive guide on personal safety, self-protection, confidence, and advocacy for young people; *Bullying: What Adults Need to Know and Do To Keep Kids Safe*, which is used in the anti-bullying programs of many families, schools, and youth organizations; and the cartoon-illustrated *Kidpower Safety Comics Series* and *Preschool to Young Adult Curriculum Teaching Books*, which provide entertaining and effective tools for introducing and practicing safety skills with young people.

About The Illustrator

Amanda Golert is an experienced self-defense instructor, trainer, passionate advocate for personal safety for children and other vulnerable people, the Center Director of Kidpower Sweden—and she also likes to draw!

For over 15 years, Amanda has supported the growth and development of Kidpower Teenpower Fullpower International. She works in partnership with Irene to illustrate, edit, and design the Kidpower cartoon books and many other educational materials.

CPSIA information can be obtained
at www.ICGtesting.com
Printed in the USA
FSOW04n0036020616
21002FS